IMAGES
of America

RHODE ISLAND'S
MILL VILLAGES
SIMMONSVILLE, POCASSET,
OLNEYVILLE, AND THORNTON

Tamucilli's Reunion Aug- 1929.

IMAGES
of America

RHODE ISLAND'S
MILL VILLAGES
SIMMONSVILLE, POCASSET,
OLNEYVILLE, AND THORNTON

Joe Fuoco

ARCADIA

First published 1997
Copyright © Joe Fuoco, 1997

ISBN 0-7524-0534-9

Published by Arcadia Publishing,
an imprint of the Chalford Publishing Corporation
One Washington Center, Dover, New Hampshire 03820
Printed in Great Britain

Library of Congress Cataloging-in-Publication Data applied for

Mill Villages is dedicated to the memory of my father,
Joseph Fuoco,
a mill hand (as he called himself) who worked hard all his life,
and for the most part in the textile mills
of the village called Thornton.

Contents

Acknowledgments

This book would have been impossible without the generosity and tremendous interest of the many people who allowed me access to their superb, treasured photographs. Thanks go to Mario Votolato, Mrs. Marion Crudale, Mary Fuoco, Nina Pezzullo, Rita Saccoccia, Palma De Blois, Ella di Biasio, the Mainelli family, Lorraine Reynolds, the Nickerson Community Center, Viola La Chapelle, Anthony Masi, John St. Lawrence, and the others who helped to preserve in this pictorial document of a way of life that has largely vanished.

Introduction

For over one hundred and twenty-five years mills dominated life in the little Rhode Island villages of Thornton, Simmonsville, Pocasset, and Olneyville. Nearly everybody worked in them; even those who did not benefited from their presence, for fortunes were made around the influx of people into the area, drawn by the mills.

The mills were named for their owners, and those names were stamped forever on the villages and towns. Hundreds were employed by the mills of Simmons Upper Village, nestled near the river that overflowed and drowned the village once, more than a century ago. Small, stucco mill houses remain to tell of that era, alongside the broken shards, the shattered walls of old mills built of New England stone. Simmons Lower Village, later named Thornton, a town teeming about an intersection, possessed mills named for British Royalty, Queen Victoria of England. British Hosiery (which later became Victoria Mill) stood on a mount of the same name and was built by Charles Fletcher, who christened the village of Thornton after his own village in England. Senator James Fowler Simmons built the first textile mill here in 1835.

The streets were laid out close to the mills, secure in their great shadows. One thing was certain: you would awaken at dawn in the tiny rooms of the row duplexes and the mills would be there. They were always there, sure and reliable. Work was a certainty. Hamlets like Frog City, named for the croaking denizens of its brooks, were the pockets of legend where folklore was nourished. There were the big, wide dirt roads that, once paved, would become Morgan (named for a mill owner), Plainfield, and Atwood Avenues. A half mile to the east were the big mills of Olneyville, the work places of thousands of immigrants, who lived on narrow, crisscrossing alley-like streets named Delaine, Aleppo, and Dike. Joining this, somewhere in between, was the village of Pocasset, with its mill and river of the same name, and its water tower still standing almost 200 feet high. In many places there were smaller, indeed tiny, factories, some no more than a floor and a few rooms—but mills nevertheless—with names like the Bag Mill, Fitch's Factory, the Paper Box mill, etc.

A way of life was created in the mill villages, and the people of the villages, the Italians, English, Irish, French, and Germans—everybody knew everybody—became a closeknit family. They all worked side by side in the din of mill machinery, lived side by side, gathered in yards on summer nights before bonfires to sing and talk, and went to each other's baptisms, weddings, wakes, and funerals. Their names are carved in gray slate and New England granite, locked in time, in cemeteries at the sides of old roads, near fields, in back yards. Bosses, foremen, and mule spinners, skilled and unskilled workers of all kinds, sleep the sleep of eternity together.

The mills were the core. My father Joe was a mill hand; his mother worked in a mill as well, along with his sister, brother, cousins, uncles, and aunts. Children worked there, too. Few were able to envision the mills ever falling silent, but when cheaper opportunities for manufacturing arose in the South, the textile businesses left. A way of life ended for people then in the mill villages. Many felt the emptiness of panic, of uncertainty. Others moved on to different jobs, passing the great, quiet, abandoned mills, remembering. Those mills that stand today have found other uses. They are flea markets, condos, and warehouses, holding kinds of businesses that have nothing to do with the great heyday of their flourishing. Some have burned to the ground, others are fragments, a wall here, a floor there, perhaps several empty rooms. But the memory of the characters who lived in the villages are alive, and the row houses have been modernized and restored. The streets still bear the old names—Pocasset, Mill, John, Myrtle Avenue, Custer, Plainfield, Atwood, Victoria Mount, Pezzullo, Walnut, Maple, Joy, School, Baker, Priscilla Lane, Angelica, Delaine, Harris, Aleppo—old names that remain intact.

The people who worked in the mills are mostly gone, but the few that remain remember those days well. Generations have passed into memory, yet the mills stand as testimony to the way they worked, how they worked, and what they built with such undimmed pride in their efforts.

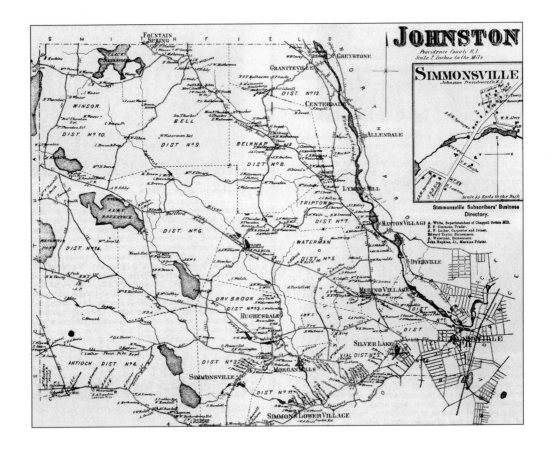

One
The Era of the Mills

Victoria Mills and its water tower. This was the mecca for so many hundreds settling in what was called Simmons Lower Village, later Thornton.

The way it looked then. The mills were already built, and the village called Thornton was growing along Main Street. Later it would shape itself about a hub at an intersection bisected by Atwood and Plainfield Streets.

An event recorded. This is the removal of the smoke stack of the Fitch Manufacturing Company on November 9, 1907. This small mill was one of many nestled in the shadow of the great mills close to the Pocasset River. (Photograph courtesy of Viola La Chapelle.)

The Pocasset Worsted Company Mill. Named after the Pocasset tribe (which had long since vanished), this mill employed 1,000 villagers at its height, during the years of two major wars. It created a fine yarn sold to other companies for weaving and knitting, and was the first company in Rhode Island to offer prizes in garden contests to the people of the mill cottages.

The Casino. Built by the owners of the Pocasset Worsted Mill, this building was used for recreation of all kinds, including bowling, pool, minstrel shows, banquets, etc. It was totally destroyed by fire in 1944.

The British Hosiery Mill, later the Priscilla Worsted Mill. One of the earliest of the large mills in the village, British Hosiery goes back to 1884. It was built in a village within a village, comically called Frog City, which remains famed to this day, having kept that name.

The row houses of the mill workers on John Street near Frog City. Once completely identical, this more contemporary photograph shows what owners have done to individualize them. These were the " company houses" built by mill owners for their employees. Coal and electricity were supplied by the owners. These houses were built for the workers of the Victoria Mills. Below them were other row houses, most of them gone, for the workers of Priscilla Mill.

12

A street procession of over fifty years ago. The Paper Box mill, as it was called, is in the distance. Sitting close to the Pocasset River that supplied its power, this small mill served the town well until it perished in a great fire several years ago. (Photograph courtesy of Mario Votolato.)

The Paper Box mill from another angle. A three-story brick and stucco building, it was the smallest mill in several villages. (Photograph courtesy of Mario Votolato.)

A horse-drawn trolley in the village. Electric trolleys came later, and the tracks remained for decades before being uprooted. This very old photograph shows an "open" car (in that it was open in the front and back). (Photograph courtesy of Mario Votolato.)

Two guys on lunch break outside of Priscilla Mill in the early 1940s. My father was a mill hand in those days; that is Joe Sr. on the left. (Photograph courtesy of Joe Fuoco.)

The Pocasset Mill. Hundreds worked here during the war spinning yarn. The water tank stands to this day. (Photograph courtesy of Mario Votolato.)

The Victoria Mill. Sprawling, the largest of the mills, this 1910s view shows the mill houses arranged close to the mill. These houses still stand and are occupied. The dirt road is John Street; the village within a village is Frog City. (Photograph courtesy of Mario Votolato.)

Plainfield Street at Atwood Avenue and Mill Street. This photograph may have been taken during a Fourth of July or the celebration of Armistice; notice the flags in the windows of the large building. These houses are still standing. (Photograph courtesy of Mario Votolato.)

A scene from 1912. This muddy road with horse and buggy tracks is Plainfield Street at its junction with Atwood Avenue. Many of the buildings made it to the 1960s and a little beyond; some remain standing. (Photograph courtesy of Mario Votolato.)

A view of the sprawling Atlantic Mills complex in Olneyville. This was the place of work of the villagers of Olneyville. A few smaller mills crowded the streets such as Aleppo Street, but this was the big mill. (Photograph courtesy of Albert J. Lothrop.)

A trolley car. This was the way people got to work, if they had to travel to the mills of Olneyville. Notice the stops, Olneyville, Dyer Avenue, and Swan Point. The latter is a sprawling cemetery, a few miles from Olneyville.

One of the remaining old houses in the village of Olneyville. Nearly dilapidated, this house, with its original shingles, goes back to the heyday of the mills. (Photograph courtesy of the Nickerson Community Center.)

A tenement house of Olneyville. Notice the small mill structure to the left, converted, and in the distance the top floor of another mill complex. (Photograph courtesy of the Nickerson Community Center.)

Two
Village People;
Mill Workers

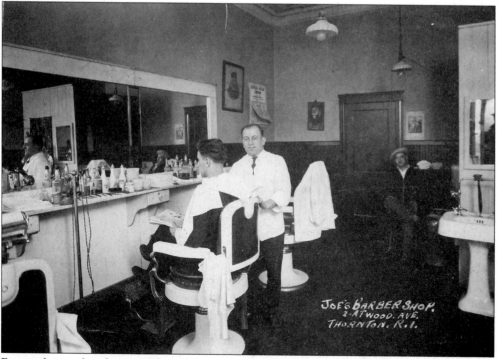

Essential as coal and water. There was never a shortage of barber shops in any mill village. Joe Croce in a spiffy shop on Plainfield Street stops for a pose while cutting a young man's hair. Notice the white bottles on the counter, unquestionably the tart, strong smelling preference of the day, Old Spice. (Photograph courtesy of Joe Croce.)

A happy-looking trio. Younger, of another generation, this group did not work in the mills. (Photograph courtesy of Joe Fuoco.)

Florine and Joe in the 1940s. Joe was a mill hand who rose to foreman. Behind them is a big cement container called an ash bin. Here the garbage of a large tenement house was deposited to rot in the open air. (Photograph courtesy of Joe Fuoco.)

Everybody called him Fuzza. A street person who slept in the wooden ice house (during the summer) near the village intersection, Fuzza was one of the town's indelible characters. Behind him is the entertainment mecca of the town, the colorful Village Rendezvous, a hotel, restaurant, and lounge. (Photograph courtesy of Mario Votolato.)

Hanging out. A group of village boys (notice the popularity of the tams) hang around on a non-working day. Gasoline sold for 10¢ a gallon—but who in the village could afford cars? Only a very few. (Photograph courtesy of Mario Votolato.)

Now that car was something, the talk of the town. This was the famed intersection of the village of Thornton, and the building behind it was the first "Mall." It housed a bowling alley, two barber shops, a deli-spa, a pool parlor, and an espresso coffee shop on the first floor; on the second floor was one of the two motion picture theatres in the village. The people here are Mike Leo (left), the owner of the pool parlor, and Mike Rainone (right), the proud owner of the convertible. (Photograph courtesy of Joe Fuoco.)

Two of the legends of Simmons Lower Village. And lucky legends they were: to the left is Joe Mendozzi, dapper, elegant, a barber who never had to work in any of the mills; to the right is Al Devine. (Photograph courtesy of Mario Votolato.)

The numerous departments of the sprawling Atlantic Mills. Here is Helen Madden at her wooden desk. She was a bookkeeper in the winding room of the Atlantic Mills. Notice the adding machine! (Photograph courtesy of Ella Di Biasio.)

Three very aristocratic-looking ladies of old Olneyville, when part of it was still in the town of Johnston. Anna Michonski Niewadonski (center) began working in the Atlantic Mill when she was eighteen years old. Her sister, Louise Michonski Beaune (left), also worked in the mill. Anna's son Paul, who lives in Cranston, remembers bringing his mother's hot lunch to the mill when he was in his early teens. (Photograph courtesy of Jamie Carter.)

Giovanni "John" Votolato, a most distinguished gentleman and the father of many children. (Photograph courtesy of Mario Votolato.)

A photo at least a century old. Enrichetta and Nicandro Viti were the parents of Mrs. Votolato, who lived into her nineties and owned the first motion picture theatre in what was then called Simmons Lower Village (present-day Thornton). The theatre, which still stands, was called the Myrtle Theatre. (Photograph courtesy of Mario Votolato.)

Five Olneyville villagers in the spinning room of the Atlantic Mills, in the days when air conditioning was a rarity. (Photograph courtesy of Ella Di Biasio.)

Louie Leo. If ever there was a legend this is one. A raconteur and inveterate walker (long before it became fashionable), Louie was a village mainstay. Immaculate and overly fussy, he was the soul of cleanliness and the brother of Mike Leo, pool parlor impresario. (Photograph courtesy of Joe Fuoco.)

Some of the townsfolk. This was the famous corner, the intersection, the hub of Atwood Avenue and Plainfield Street, where all the towns met. From left to right, standing with some majesty, are Mike Leo, Emil Fuoco (a second-generation entrepreneur), Henry D'Ambra, George Del Santo (one of the town's first insurance brokers), and Kelly Tundis. (Photograph courtesy of Joe Fuoco.)

Bars in abundance. The mill villages were characterized not only by neatly aligned row houses and narrow back streets but also by their bars, which were plentiful. Here Fred Ferri stands before the family establishment called Ferri's Tavern, one of at least five bordering an intersection. Notice that if you went in for some brew on a Friday night, you ate clams for free! The clientele of the bars along Plainfield Street came from Frog City to Olneyville. (Photograph courtesy of Joe Fuoco.)

"Buzzy" Ferri. Handsome, stylish, and successful, "Buzzy" stands on Main Street on a sunny Sunday morning. (Photograph courtesy of Joe Fuoco.)

Same intersection, different subjects. Mike Leo (left) either refuses to face the camera most of the time, or that's his good side. (Photograph courtesy of Joe Fuoco.)

A scene lost forever. The signs are gone, the tree is gone, the cars are gone. This is Anthony "Handsome" Ferri with his son Anthony Jr. Everybody called him "Handsome" for he owned one of the barber shops in the village. Something called "crank case service" was still offered by the local gas station when this photograph was taken. (Photograph courtesy of Joe Fuoco.)

Al and Emil in front of the Village Rendezvous, famed for its bronze handles on the doors. The Village Rendezvous was *the* mecca for entertainment. (Photograph courtesy of Joe Fuoco.)

George Hall, a boss at the Atlantic Mills. Nobody could look this dour unless he had a bad day. That office could use some remodeling! (Photograph courtesy of Ella Di Biasio.)

A family portrait of the Santurri's. Mother Filomena was a worker in the mills for many years. Father Cleofido also worked in the Atlantic Mills in Olneyville. Children Nina and Eddy probably never saw the inside of a mill, but prospered. (Photograph courtesy of Nina Pezzullo.)

Florine Tella at seventeen. One of the loveliest girls of Pocasset Village, Florine was a soprano in the local church. A second-generation villagite, she and her large family (five sisters, one brother) enjoyed the benefits of education when many of the village did not go beyond grammar school. (Photograph courtesy of Joe Fuoco.)

Workers of the Thornton Worsted Mills, later known as Pocasset Mill, the big mill of Pocasset Village. The identity of this quintet is lost in time, with the exception of Tommy Taylor at the extreme left. (Photograph courtesy of Viola La Chapelle.)

A 1930s steam shovel on what would become Plainfield Pike. Pictured are Nick Barone, superintendent Eddie Young, and Mike Musharon. As the villages grew and spread, and as many townsfolk became able to afford houses or built tenements, a whole new work force was created, one other than that which staffed the mills. (Photograph courtesy of Joe Croce.)

The wedding of John Tella (also known as Jack Taylor) to Rose Iannuccilli, eighty-five years ago. Patrician looking, they met in the choir loft of the old St. Rocco Church, married, and had nine children. It was John's father, Daniel Tella, who, one day after work in the little mill near the Pocasset River in Thornton, crossed a threshold and suffered a massive coronary. John was the finest tenor in the village. (Photograph courtesy of Viola La Chapelle.)

One of the first all-round stores in the village of Thornton (Simmons Lower): Mainelli's Spa. This store was and is to this day a magnet. The photograph, taken in 1936, shows Mike (the owner, on the left) with his wife Mamie and their sons Nick and Al. (Photograph courtesy of Joe Fuoco.)

A more recent photograph. Nick, Mamie, and Al are shown here in Mainelli's, on the same spot. Mamie has since passed away, but the store, which has been open for more than sixty years, is still operating, having become a village staple. (Photograph courtesy of Joe Fuoco.)

She was known as Rosina L'Inglese, and she is the true definition of the Mill Village citizen. Born in Dublin, Ireland, of Irish and Italian parents, Rose Bassi came to America, the wife of Andino Fuoco. She lived all her life and died in a mill house on John Street. Working in the Victoria Mill at the end of her street, she spoke with a soft brogue. Rose bore three of her four children in the mill house, and was forever known as Rose the Englishwoman, though not a drop of English blood flowed through her veins. (Photograph courtesy of Joe Fuoco.)

Standing on the corner. You can almost hear the song playing. Anthony of the barber shop is on the right; Joe is on the left. A haircut was 75¢, a buck with a tip. (Photograph courtesy of Joe Fuoco.)

A young immigrant family of Simmons Lower Village/Thornton. The street behind them is John Street, and the house sits at the corner of a street of row houses. The grapevine behind speaks of another country, a custom brought to the new world. The people are Ella, little Ralph, and Albert Martinelli. (Photograph courtesy of Marion Crudale.)

Anthony "Swede" Lanni in a classic pose, near what is now a very classic car. Nearby is a Thornton village club where cards were dealt and bets were made. (Photograph courtesy of Mario Votolato.)

Five characters, each a study in individuality. What a group, always looking as if they were dressed for an event. These men represent at least three villages and as many generations. (Photograph courtesy of Mario Votolato.)

A memorable portrait at the corner of the village. This was where the roads crossed, which made it a perfect place for villagers to assemble. Just look at the dapper Don on the right. What a look! (Photograph courtesy of Mario Votolato.)

"China." Vincent Salzillo owned "China's." If your car broke down, if you needed a grease job or an oil change, this is where you came. He repaired more cars than he could remember. (Photograph courtesy of Mario Votolato.)

One of the traditional gathering spots, in front of China's gasoline station. Everybody sat here. The view included the intersection, the roofs of the mills, one of the churches, and just about everybody who lived in the area. From left to right are Eddie Mendozzi (who later became the town chief of police), "Crack" Branca, Frank Croce, and "Swede" Lanni. (Photograph courtesy of Mario Votolato.)

Ro-Ro. Everybody called her Ro-Ro, and they still do. A daughter of a very large family, who all worked at one time or another in the Priscilla and Victoria Mills, Ro-Ro is shown here standing by her fence before a slate-sided mill house on John Street. (Photograph courtesy of Marion Crudale.)

A family of the mills. Notice the grape arbor and the lush garden to the right. The street nearby is John Street, marked by row houses. (Photograph Courtesy of Marion Crudale.)

Anna Pansera, nee Anna Martinelli. A tough, feisty, outspoken woman of great strength, she worked in the mills of Lower Simmons and Pocasset Village and Atlantic Mills of Olneyville all her life, tirelessly, and kept a cellar miraculously stocked with preserves of every kind. (Photograph courtesy of Marion Crudale.)

Young Jenny Martinelli. The house of whitewashed cement blocks stands to this day on Plainfield Street, near John Street (where row houses still remain). Jenny worked hard in the mills. So did her husband Joe. (Photograph courtesy of Marion Crudale.)

Anna Pansera in the family yard with her infant daughter Marion. Anna rose to become a boss in the mill called Priscilla. (Photograph courtesy of Marion Crudale.)

Elegant mill workers. When they dressed up, they didn't fool around. These were not rich people, but there is still an elegance, a sense of decorum, and look at the corsages. (Photograph courtesy of Marion Crudale.)

Ella Di Biasio, who undoubtedly had one of the better jobs at the Atlantic Mills, Olneyville Village. She was a secretary, and a neat one. Notice the old telephone on her desk. (Photograph courtesy of Ella Di Biasio.)

Workers in the textile mills of Olneyville. Women who had worked in the textile mills during World War II continued working for some time after the war ended. Notice the characteristic headband of the 1940s on the woman to the left, and the rows of yarn spools. (Photograph courtesy of Ella Di Biasio.)

A quintet of mill workers at the Atlantic Mills, Olneyville. The war is over, and they are working without pressure. In fact, they seem to be enjoying it. (Photograph courtesy of Ella Di Biasio.)

The John "Jack" Reynolds Garage on Mill Street. There is Jack playing rough with a young friend. The Reynolds family was one of the more well known of the English families in the mill town. John's wife May, a quick, fiery, hard worker, labored in the Priscilla Mill, directly across the street from this garage. Up the street was the Victoria Mill. (Photograph courtesy of Lorraine Reynolds.)

Two lovely young women. The woman to the right is enjoying a day off from the spinning spools of the Atlantic Mills. Her friend does not look as if she had ever worked in an Olneyville Mill. (Photograph courtesy of the Nickerson Community Center.)

Three
There Were Weddings
. . . and Wars

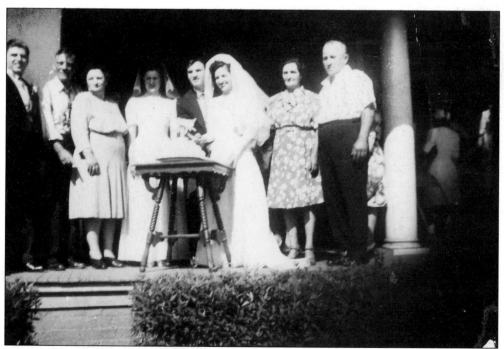

The wedding of Viola Tella to Rudolph La Chapelle. On the stairs of the casino built by English mill owners for the pleasure of their workers, a family celebrates a union in Pocasset Village. (Photograph courtesy of Joe Fuoco.)

The wedding of Nicholas Masi and Minnie DiLullo. "Nick" worked in the factories. He lost most of his left arm in a mill accident but for the rest of his life his dexterity was amazing. (Photograph courtesy of Anthony Masi.)

The mother of the bride. Beautiful Filomena Santurri, who lived in a mill house at the edge of Simmons Lower/Thornton for nearly her entire life, worked in the local mills. Her mother, called Rosina L'Inglese, was one of the legends of Frog City, and her daughter Nina was called the most beautiful girl in town. (Photograph courtesy of Joe Fuoco.)

Nina Santurri, a child of mill workers who never had to work in a mill. Elegant, beautiful, many thought she was the local Betty Grable. There is an amazing resemblance. (Photograph courtesy of Joe Fuoco.)

The wedding of Nina Santurri, the most beautiful girl in town. Emerging from one half of a row house, escorted by her father Cleofido, the bride walks toward John Street. This is an out of a row house wedding. Neighbors and children watch. (Photograph courtesy of Joe Fuoco.)

Father and daughter pose just before getting into a limo. Notice the false brick of the millhouse. Once the row houses were all one color. Later, individual owners added their own touches. (Photograph courtesy of Joe Fuoco.)

Coming down the historic steps of St. Rocco Church. The church was built by immigrants to the three villages, from as far north as Hughesdale, a village within a village called Simmonsville. Nina Santurri, now Nina Pezzullo, emerges a married woman. (Photograph courtesy of Joe Fuoco.)

The bride and groom, Mr. and Mrs. Raymond J. Pezzullo. She's as radiant as a queen, and he's filled with confidence. He went on to become the first dentist to take up practice in the village, in the big mansion with the Ionic columns called the Simmons house. (Photograph courtesy of Joe Fuoco.)

And another brother marries. Michael Iannuccilli, who developed the Victoria Greenhouses in the shadow of the Victoria Mill, married Ethel Evans. They are the couple on the left. (Photograph courtesy of Viola La Chapelle.)

The wedding of Bennie Iannuccilli to Christina Fuoco. Christina worked in various mills, and Bennie, "shell-shocked" in World War I, kept gardens known for their variety of roses. (Photograph courtesy of Viola La Chapelle.)

Two little darling sisters. Florine and Dorothy Tella, two of the children of John and Rose Tella of Pocasset Village, are these well-behaved flower girls of some seventy-five years ago. The wedding was of an aunt and uncle, Bennie and Christina Iannuccilli of the clan in the large family portrait of 1929. (Photograph courtesy of Joe Fuoco.)

John and Rose Tella on the stairs of the old St. Rocco Church during a wedding of one of their daughters. Behind them are relatives, sisters-in-law, and a daughter. John, a master mechanic and a superb tenor, met Rose in the choir. She was briefly a mill worker, but retired after their marriage to raise six children out of nine and build a bungalow in Pocasset Village. Three of their children died in infancy. (Photograph courtesy of Joe Fuoco.)

Mr and Mrs. John Tella with their daughter Anna on the lawn of the casino, which burned to the ground in the 1940s. (Photograph courtesy of Joe Fuoco.)

The wedding of Tina Vitale and Vinnie Schiano. The only son in a large family, Vinnie and his sisters operated the largest meat market in the village that was part Pocasset, part Thornton. (Photograph courtesy of Joe Fuoco.)

Vinnie Schiano in his trusty and essential apron, on the bridge over the Pocasset River. Behind him is the tall smoke stack of the Pocasset Mill. The river powered this mill and also the smaller, stucco-paper box mill. When Vinnie went into the service, his sisters ran the market. (Photograph courtesy of Mario Votolato.)

The wedding of two from different villages. The groom, Joseph Fuoco, was a mill hand in the Priscilla Mill and lived on John Street. He was raised in a mill house. The bride is Florine Tella of Pocasset Village, an operatic singer and pianist. Years later, they moved to the center of the villages, to Thornton, once called Simmons Lower. Thus, they typified real village people. (Photograph courtesy of Joe Fuoco.)

Rosina L'Inglese, the mother of two soldiers, . She stands in the driveway of her row house. It was where she raised her children and it was where she died. (Photograph courtesy of Joe Fuoco.)

The wedding of Ella Bernardoni and Anthony Ferri. They were of well-to do, important families of Simmons Lower Village and Thornton. Notice the luxurious bouquets and the long train of Ella's magnificent gown. (Photograph courtesy of Mary Fuoco.)

The mill villages of Simmonsville-Thornton-Pocasset during the war years. Many went, and some died. Here is Joe Ricci, a survivor, in 1942. (Photograph courtesy of Mario Votolato.)

A rather handsome and determined quartet. Notice the military stances of all. From left to right are Edmund Santurri, Joe Vacca, Nicholas Ferri, and Al Vacca, standing in the heart of the village, close to a memorial to the fallen. (Photograph courtesy of Joe Fuoco.)

M. Wilson. He too survived. The graceful palm tree behind him hints of a luxurious time. But the barrel on the ground suggests something ominous. (Photograph courtesy of Mario Votolato.)

Another daughter of John Tella is given "away." Here, daughter Evelyn becomes Mrs. Michael Gesualdi. (Photograph courtesy of Joe Fuoco.)

Louis Fuoco. The youngest son of Rosina L'Inglese, Louis left his home and went into the army. For years after returning from World War II his uniform hung in the upstairs closet, in the garret of the mill house. (Photograph courtesy of Joe Fuoco.)

Annie Scungio, with a fake brick-faced row house behind her. All dressed up for a wedding, Annie lived in one of the oldest houses anywhere, made of stone and cement blocks. (Photograph courtesy of Marion Crudale.)

A wedding out of a row house. Antonio Fuoco escorts his daughter Nettie on her wedding day. (Photograph courtesy of Marion Crudale.)

Sweethearts? Maybe, maybe not. Nettie and an unknown suitor, or friend, or maybe even relative, in the '40s. Behind them a row house of old-fashioned slate siding. (Photograph courtesy of Marion Crudale.)

Rose (Ro-Ro, left) and her sister Nettie (right) in front of their mill house, where their mother Carrie raised so many children. Obviously bridesmaids, they were soon to become brides themselves. (Photograph courtesy of Marion Crudale.)

Mary and Emil Fuoco. It was never easy to say goodbye, especially after a furlough. Here the former Mary Ferri hugs her soldier-husband Emil before he goes back to his base. (Photograph courtesy of Mary Fuoco.)

Frank Scungio and one of his daughters. Everybody called him "Stubby." He is shown here escorting one of his daughters from a row house on her wedding day. Even through the heavy veil it looks like Margaret. (Photograph courtesy of Marion Crudale.)

Lillian Votolato. The town's first school nurse, Lillian left for a while during the war years. Her family, a most illustrious one in the village, was not of the mills, but was surrounded by them. The villages also produced their aristocracy. (Photograph courtesy of Mario Votolato.)

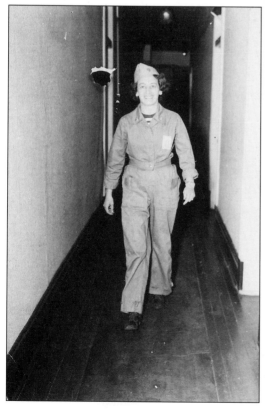

A proud Nancy Votolato in her service uniform. (Photograph courtesy of Mario Votolato.)

Soldiers from the village. Frank Fuoco (left) and an unidentified pal stand very stoically near an army truck. Frank lived all his life on Joy Street, in the area of three major mills: Victoria, Priscilla, and British Hosiery. His five sisters worked in the mill. (Photograph courtesy of John St. Lawrence.)

Two sailors and a pretty girl. Sounds like a 1940s movie title. Annie, then Annie Fuoco, stands between her cousin, Angelo Vitale (left), and an unidentified friend on the right. The location is the family homestead on Joy Street in the village within a village comically called Frog City. The people of Frog City worked in *all* of the mills. (Photograph courtesy of John St. Lawrence.)

Home on leave. Two sailors pose with a Joy Street family. From left to right are Manuele Vitale, his wife Rose, her sister Annie, brother Frank, sister Sadie, and two neighbors. The women were the mill workers. The young men went to the war. (Photograph courtesy of John St. Lawrence.)

A wedding during World War II. Mary Fuoco and her husband, Arthur St. Lawrence, pose on the stairs of the old St. Rocco Church. Behind them are Mary's sister Melia, and her husband Frank (Turk). And the sailor, of course, is only brother Frank. (Photograph courtesy of John St. Lawrence.)

The Ferri Brothers, Anthony "Buffy" Ferri (left) and brother Nicholas (right). Both went to World War II and returned safely. They then became school principals. Part of the aristocracy of the mill village of Lower Simmons/Thornton, these soldiers were members of a large family that left a strong imprint on the life of the village. (Photograph courtesy of MAry Fuoco.)

War workers. Workers were needed on the homefront during World War II. Even as the war ended, many women remained in the mills. (Photograph courtesy of Ella Di Biasio.)

Four
Kids . . .
and More Kids

The children of mill workers—well fed, happy, and generally good kids. This group is also well dressed. (Photograph courtesy of Marion Crudale.)

Another look at the sprawling child population of the mill villages of Thornton, Pocasset, Simmonsville, etc. Saturday morning was the big day for these kids at the Myrtle Hall Theatre (still standing). They were all members of the Popeye club, which did not necessarily mean they liked their spinach. (Photograph courtesy of Mario Votolato.)

A shy little girl. Anna Masi was known for her curls. It was her dad, Nick, who lost his arm in a factory accident. (Photograph courtesy of Anthony Masi.)

Little Anna and a friend on a doorstep of a very old house close to the paper box mill. (Photograph courtesy of Anthony Masi.)

A century-old interior view of a workroom in the old Victoria Mills. Notice the ancient machinery and the bales of cotton in the distance. (Photograph courtesy of Rita Saccoccio.)

Another crowd at Myrtle Hall. The Popeye Club of 1939 was already twenty years old, and its membership was formidable. By now, of course, talking pictures were established, and even early color films had been shown on the authentic silver screen of Myrtle Hall. Everybody came

here. The hall was used for weddings, showers, banquets, minstrels—just about everything of a social nature. (Photograph courtesy of Mario Votolato.)

The legendary Dead End Kids? Do they look too solemn? They shouldn't. Here are, from left to right, Joey, Bobby, and Harold. Their parents worked in the mills. Later, Harold and Bobby Crossley, brothers, were distinguished by their mother's gutsy opening of Rose's Snack Bar, a little restaurant. (Photograph courtesy of Joe Fuoco.)

Two waifs of Olneyville, c. 1930. The mills were in full swing, and these children spent a lot of time at a settlement house on Delaine Street. (Photograph courtesy of the Nickerson Community Center.)

Enjoying the sun in old Olneyville. We do not know who this child is. The clapboard house behind her remains intact. (Photograph courtesy of Joe Fuoco.)

Children of mill workers. The Pocasset Mill is to their right. On a day such as this the din of the mill would be deafening, constant until the whistle would mercifully blow at 4 pm. (Photograph courtesy of Joe Fuoco.)

Tiny Linda, not much bigger than her doll. Her father, a mill hand named Joe who had worked his way to foreman, earned enough to buy his own home. (Photograph courtesy of Joe Fuoco.)

Three musketeers: Steve, Tommy, and Kenny. The fathers of these three hellions worked in the mills and in the boiling foundry close to Victoria Mill as well as the Atlantic Mills of Olneyville. (Photograph courtesy of Joe Fuoco.)

The one school in the village—Thornton School. Later, called Thornton Jr. High, it graduated this class in 1940. Its teacher, Nicholas Ferri, of a prominent family, left the village within three years to go to war. He returned safely and became a principal. His was a resounding success story. Notice the demure, ladylike poses of the girls, with not a spiked hair in the group. (Photograph courtesy of Mary Fuoco.)

Marion Pansera in front of the field stone paper box mill. Notice the Richfield gasoline sign in the distance, the center of the village beyond. The Pocasset River flowed next to the mill, powering it. The river still flows, but the mill is gone, a casualty to fire. (Photograph courtesy of Marion Crudale.)

Two children, Michael De Petrillo and Arthur St. Lawrence, in the snow. Behind them is the Victoria Mill, situated on Victoria Mount. (Photograph courtesy of John St. Lawrence.)

Little one-year-old Palma Scungio. She is sitting on the stairs of the family home on John Street, although she was raised just across the street in a row house. Notice the graceful railings and supports of the porch. (Photograph courtesy of Palma De Blois.)

The Day Nursery (what we now call Day Care) on Delaine Street in Olneyville. This was part of a novel program initiated by a sympathetic minister who felt the oppression and near abandonment of children whose parents worked into the night in the Olneyville mills. (Photograph courtesy of the Nickerson Community Center.)

Little Arthur Reynolds of the well-known Reynolds family. Here he sits at a wooden desk in the old Thornton School. (Photograph courtesy of Lorraine Reynolds.)

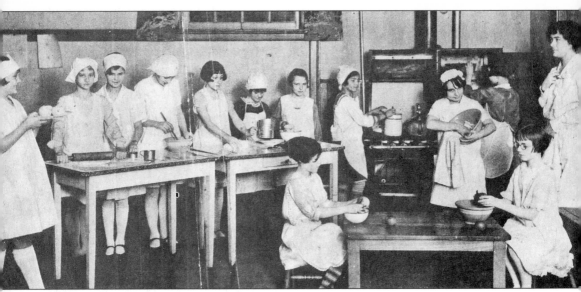

A scene from 1928. Olneyville children enjoy a very domestically oriented after-school class at a settlement house. The room looks downright antiseptic. (Photograph courtesy of the Nickerson Community Center.)

Palma Scungio as a little girl. Her parents lived in a row house on John Street and they worked in the Priscilla Mill on Mill Street. Palma herself worked in the mill as a young woman. (Photograph courtesy of Palma De Blois.)

Arthur Reynolds, a little older. They had heroes on sweat shirts in those days, too. Arthur's pullover features Tom Mix, a cowboy who made more than two hundred films. *He* was the hero. (Photograph courtesy of Lorraine Reynolds.)

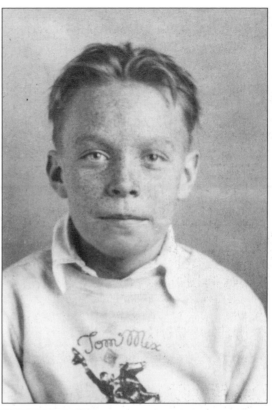

Pius Pansera and little Marion. Pius, who along with his wife Anna worked in the mills all his long life, sits in the sun against a stone house, reminiscent of the stone houses of Italy. (Photograph courtesy of Marion Crudale.)

Myrtle Hall. It looks as if the entire child population of the four mill villages is here, and it may be a fact. They're everywhere, even in the windows. Kids came from the surrounding towns for this event. Myrtle Hall, still standing, was one of two motion picture theatres not far from the intersection of Atwood and Plainfield, half-way between Pocasset and Thornton. And Saturdays were club days. Talking films were in their infancy or not yet invented. This historic photograph comes courtesy of Thomas Fuoco.

The Thornton Grammar School. A stately, almost Gothic building, it was one of two schools in the village. The first, still standing and now a private dwelling, was a one-room schoolhouse. This large school, built in 1892, burned on January 13, 1919. Later, a new school was built, and is still standing.

Five

The Church in the Village

The church named for a legendary Irish saint, Brigid. Built in 1914, this church served the immigrant Irish laborers who worked in the Pocasset Mill across the street and the other mills of Olneyville and Simmonsville, and who lived in the row houses of Walnut Street, Pocasset Street, Maple Avenue, and Spruce Street (most named for the trees that abounded in the area).

The interior of the first ethnic church in the old village of Simmonsville Lower and Thornton. The St. Rocco Church, built in 1903, was the Italian church, so called, for it was built with the sweat and toil of Italian mill workers and those in private business. Ornate, reflecting the style of a southern Italian village, it was in use until 1950, when the new church was built. (Photograph courtesy of Anthony Masi.)

The Congregational church nearly one hundred years ago. To serve the English settlers, mill owners, workers, and their families years before the Italian and Irish immigrants arrived, the Church of the Epiphany (Episcopal) and this church, simply called the Congregational Church of Thornton, were built. The buildings to the left still remain, but the church is gone. Where it stood is a restaurant, itself over sixty years old. (Photograph courtesy of Al and Nicholas Mainelli.)

A photograph, dating from the end of the nineteenth century, of a group of villagers in front of the famed Simmons Mansion. Simmons village was named for this cotton mill owner. Later, this magnificent house became the dwelling of the Pezzullo family. All about was a great farm. The house today is intact, but the farms have become avenues and paved streets. (Photograph courtesy of Rita Saccoccio.)

An outing in 1939. The Pocasset, Victoria, Priscilla, and the Atlantic Mills, etc. employed many of the mill workers in this photo graph. Those who are not mill workers belonged to a very unique group of senators, store owners, etc. (Photograph courtesy of Rita Saccoccio.)

Another confirmation day. This one belonging to Nicholina Ferri, standing next to her godmother Mary Fuoco. The Ferri family, a true force in the town, was prominent in business, in the school department, and in the life of the village. They owned a block containing several businesses and also owned a theatre, a sports field, taverns, etc. (Photograph courtesy of Joe Fuoco.)

Anthony Masi and his sponsor, his godfather Gile Arruda. Confirmations were important in those days, and usually took place around the age of thirteen. It was Anthony's father who lost his arm in a mill accident. (Photograph courtesy of Anthony Masi.)

Grace Memorial House.

dedicated Dec 17-1885 by Bishop Clark.

An old sketch of the Grace Memorial House, which would later be transformed into a sprawling settlement house. Grace Church, a stone structure, eventually became one of the major houses of worship in Olneyville. (Photograph courtesy of Nickerson Community Center.)

On their way to church, or coming back. Standing on Plainfield Street near a small store are, from left to right, Rae Ferri, Anna Pansera, and Antoniella Ricci, all memorable people of the town. Rae worked in the tavern as a waitress for many years, Anna worked all her life in the mill, and Antoniella, carrying her homemade biscuits, went from house to house visiting the sick. There was barely a house she missed. (Photograph courtesy of Joe Fuoco.)

All dressed up with definitely someplace to go. Mary St. Lawrence, baton twirler extraordinary, poses regally before a parade is about to begin. Behind her is a two-decker mill house. Mary and her sisters worked in the Priscilla Mill and retired while still working there more than fifty years later. (Photograph courtesy of John St. Lawrence.)

A little girl, Marie La Chapelle, after her First Holy Communion. She stands between her proud grandparents, John and Rose Tella of Pocasset Village It was John's father who, more than forty years before, stepped from the paper box mill one day near the Pocasset River, after work, and suddenly fell, dead, of a heart attack. The story was known everywhere. (Photograph courtesy of Joe Fuoco.)

One of the oldest pictures in existence of the St. Rocco Church. This structure was a mecca for the faithful of all the villages who professed the Roman Catholic faith. Look at the size of this early parish. The photograph dates from about 1902. (Photograph courtesy of Mary Fuoco.)

Expressions of relief. These kids won't have to walk the several miles of the procession. How they escaped it is anybody's guess. (Photograph courtesy of Joe Fuoco.)

A significant day at St. Rocco Church. How far had a mill village developed by the 1950s? Here is pictorial proof, for none other than a Rhode Island Bishop, Russel J. McVinney complete with miter, descends the stairs of the basilica-like St. Rocco Church on a feast day. (Photograph courtesy of Joe Fuoco.)

Six
Some Good Times

A variety show in Olneyville, at the Nickerson House. The kids are rehearsing for a show appropriately called *Your Hit Parade*. (Photograph courtesy of Nickerson Community Center.)

A gathering of the big guys, village politicians at the Village Rendezvous, one of the five or six "watering places" at the intersection. In this room are councilmen, future leaders, wardsmen, and monied supporters. Notice the sign under the fan. It reads "Try our Paradise Special 25 cents." Now that was some drink! (Photograph courtesy of Joe Croce.)

John J. Connsellor of Hong Kong. Nobody knows who he was, but on September 30, 1929, he was honored by townsfolk in Myrtle Hall. (Photograph courtesy of Mario Votolato.)

And the band played on. One of the oldest pictures surviving from the mill era, this was a local band that played concerts during feasts, setting up a band stand or marching through the streets. (Photograph courtesy of Mario Votolato.)

John Tella (known as Jack Taylor), a soccer and baseball player, well-known tenor, and master mechanic on Packard cars. Here he is about twenty-one years old. John went to the one-room schoolhouse on the Pike. (Photograph courtesy of Joe Fuoco.)

A fete for Albert R. Tavani in 1938. Many of the people in this splendid photograph were mill workers, or the descendants of mill workers, who "made good" and became cultural, economic, and political forces in the community. The occasion? Albert R. Tavani had been admitted to the RI Bar; everybody was there, representing several mill towns. Seated at the table to the right, eight people in, is John O. Pastore, now in his nineties. He became governor, then senator, and gave the keynote address at the Democratic National Convention. (Photograph courtesy of Mario Votolato.)

A parade about to begin—an image that defines the time. Politicians and dignitaries are on the band stand, while children watch from the ground below. This nearly 100-year-old photograph is virtually a historical document. The sign on the building just under the flag says "First Class Boot and Shoe Maker." That was the only way to go! (Photograph courtesy of Mario Votolato.)

The Victoria Athletic Club of 1907, named for Victoria Mill and Victoria Mount. From left to right are as follows: (front row) John Simone, "John Doe" (his face is unidentifiable), Mr. Carrier, Pat La Fazia, and Tommy Buffo; (middle row) Mike Perry, Mr. Delmonte, and Tony Votolato; (back row) John Tella (Jack Taylor), Jack Canuff, Tony Sport, and Tommy Taylor. (Photograph courtesy of Joe Fuoco.)

An early baseball team—the Thornton Champs. When people begin to prosper, and when they work together in a small area, they play together as well, and the family of the town grows. (Photograph courtesy of Mario Votolato.)

What kids do this today. Here are Olneyville kids enjoying the summer playing at what is called a playground puzzle table. The time is the 1930s. (Photograph courtesy of the Nickerson Community Center.)

209. Camp Hamilton. This camp was created for the children of Olneyville village, and here is a somewhat neat line of them, enjoying what they did not have in a crowded, air-thickened mill village. (Photograph courtesy of the Nickerson Community Center.)

Fitness in the 1930s. This group of young women is struggling to remain fit at the Nickerson Community Center, Olneyville. In those clothes, it's hard to tell who's in good shape and who isn't. (Photograph courtesy of the Nickerson Community Center.)

Members of the Community Club at an outing in the early 1930s. Thornton enjoyed quite a social life. Note the knickers on the man to the left. That was considered "sharp" in those days. (Photograph courtesy of Mario Votolato.)

What a bowling team! In this throng are mill hands, superintendents, a senator, and a florist—some of the poorest and richest members of the village. Many came from the garrets of the row houses; a few from mansions. (Photograph courtesy of Joe Croce.)

Sports, and more sports! Here is a soccer team in conference. The august gentleman facing us is definitely not the coach. He is Herb Murray, lover of soccer. (Photograph courtesy of Mario Votolato.)

So they put on a show, these kids of Olneyville. Here are some budding Judys, Mickeys, and Shirleys. (Photograph courtesy Nickerson Community Center.)

The allure of stardom. Everybody wants to be on stage—everybody, especially this would be Frank Sinatra from Olneyville. One wonders if he really made it! (Photograph courtesy of the Nickerson Community Center.)

The Thornton Veteran's Team, 1946–47. Just after the war, the lucky ones of the villages who came home were eager to engage in a more human kind of combat, on the sports field. Many of these guys are still around with strong memories of the war years and the peacetime that followed. From left to right are as follows: (front row) Joe Criscuolo, Vincent "Flat" Jacavony, Mario "Cowboy" Ardente, Frank "Blinkhorn" Ricci, Louie "Buster" Jacavony, and Al Vacca; (middle row) Joe Macera, Mike "Buck" Mendozzi, Joe Vacca, Anthony "Swede" Landi, and Lenny "Seaweed" Macari; (back row) Tommy Gargano, Anthony "Snub" Ricci, Johnny Macari, Louie "Brave" Alviano, Ralph "Tattoo" Muscatelli, Edo Macari, and Pat Palumbo. (Photograph courtesy of Anthony Landi.)

A soccer team. This team was composed entirely of young men of the town, though they took the name Cranston, which was the "city next door." (Photograph courtesy of Mario Votolato.)

Summer outings. The Tella family of Pocasset Village poses at one of the parks, possibly Goddard Park or Oakland Beach. The latter was destroyed in the hurricane of '38. (Photograph courtesy of Joe Fuoco.)

Three mill village beauties. No, they were not baton twirlers, that was only an act. Behind them is the "new" St. Rocco Church, of which they seem delightfully disinterested. (Photograph courtesy of Joe Fuoco.)

A summer cookout. Here are mill hands, barbers, newsstand owners, neighbors, and good friends. (Photograph courtesy of Joe Fuoco.)

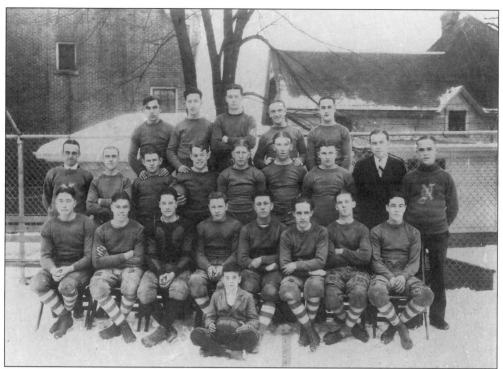

The Nickerson House Football team. Known as the Nickerson Tigers, they seemed a determined lot when this photograph was taken on Saturday, December 18, 1926! (Photograph courtesy of the Nickerson Community Center.)

A mill family. But for one, these brothers and one sister were all mill workers who put in their early years in the Victoria and Priscilla Mills. From left to right are Emil and Joe Fuoco, sister Filomena Santurri, and the youngest brother Louis, who escaped the factory. (Photograph courtesy of Joe Fuoco.)

The Swing Haven Canteen in the early 1950s. There was really no close dancing here, at least not that close. Mario Votolato and his wife Ann ran a tight ship, no nonsense, and once you were inside there was no sneaking away. No parent in the town ever had to "check up" on Saturday nights. Their kids were at Swing Haven. (Photographs courtesy of Mario Votolato.)

Mario at the drums. Not only was Mario Votolato the top gun of the Swing Haven Canteen, he was also its drummer. On the stage of Myrtle Hall , where once a silver screen hung for silents and talkies, Mario accompanied recordings or just did his own playing while the kids danced. (Photograph courtesy of Mario Votolato.)

The Swing Haven Canteen. How many social functions, how many faces did the old Myrtle Theatre have? It served as a silent movie house, talking film motion picture theatre, hall, and canteen. In the 1940s, following the end of World War II, Mario Votolato and his wife Ann formed the Swing Haven Canteen, which was for decades the place for the youth of the town to dance, court (always carefully chaperoned and observed), and meet their future mates. So it was in the village. And here, in 1947, are some of the canteen members, too young for the war that had just ended, but old enough for another that would begin in a few years. (Photograph courtesy of Mario Votolato.)

The interior of the Johnston Theatre. Where did the mill workers go, and where did they send their children on Saturday mornings? To the "show." Everybody went to the show. When Myrtle Theatre stopped showing movies, the Johnston Theatre was the setting where Nyoka the Jungle Girl replaced Pearl White, and Maria Montez danced with an enormous fake snake. You could "make the dish" there, meaning that each week one piece of a set of dishes was given to a patron until a whole set was completed. There was a community—a family—feeling that passed with the demolition of the block that housed the theatre. (Picture collection of Joe Fuoco.)

The canteen in December 1952. With a war raging in a strange, oriental land, Santa Claus came and stood before a scrawny tree. The little boy looks uncertain; the little girl looks either indifferent or distracted. (Photograph courtesy of Mario Votolato.)

So she's too big for Santa Claus to pick up. She is still a winner of something, or so it appears. Take a gander at that Santa Claus mask . Today it might be called politically correct. (Photograph courtesy of Mario Votolato.)

Three Thornton-ites at a pin ball machine. Vincent Lanni, holding the cue stick, is joined by Louis Alviano (center) and Anthony "Swede" Landi. Lanni's parents walked to and from the mills each day through the war years. (Photograph courtesy of Mario Votolato.)

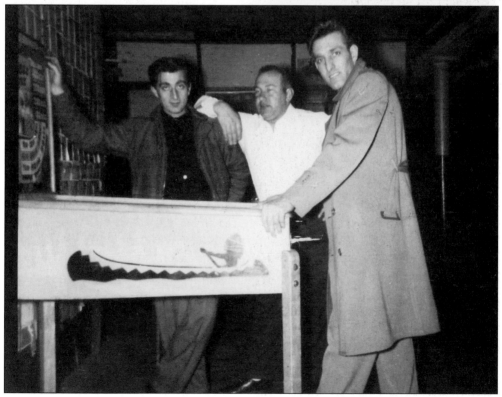

A "V" for Victory—soccer players in the 1920s. (Photograph courtesy Mario Votolato.)

Christmas in Olneyville. That tree must be 10 feet high, making the star probably 12 feet high! The Community Center of Olneyville, on Delaine Street, offered much to the kids of this mill village. (Photograph courtesy of the Nickerson Community Center.)

A big gathering of Olneyville folk in the gymnasium at the Nick, as it was called. Olneyville's period of tremendous growth was eventually followed by a decline in population, as hundreds moved away from the congested mill center. (Photograph courtesy of the Nickerson Community Center.)

The big night in Olneyville, a Saturday night dance. Notice the harmless refreshments listed, even cola with a "K." (Photograph courtesy of the Nickerson Community Center.)

VICTORY BANQUET BY
AND JOHNSTO
NARRAGANSETT HOT

A victory celebration. Now this was a gathering. The villages of Simmonsville, Thornton, Pocasset, and later Olneyville, when the English aristocracy lost their clout, had but one political party to speak of in the 1930s, and that was the Democratic Party. This was the New

Deal era. The mills were gearing up for a war yet to be fought, but perhaps inevitable. This veritable throng celebrates a victory, and not at all a surprising one. (Photograph courtesy of Joe Fuoco.)

A Christmas celebration of Priscilla Mill workers. The table is ample, the workers seem happy. The time is December 1951—just before another war. But for this day, the machinery literally ground to a halt. There certainly were flanges from the days of the sweat factories. Notice the lighting, windows, etc. (Photographs courtesy of Marion Crudale.)

The old bandstand in daylight. Here, on a Saturday night, the eve of a feast day, a band played opera selections and old waltzes. The village came out and listened. (Photograph courtesy of Mario Votolato.)

The bandstand at night. This remarkable very old photograph is clear enough to detail a Ferris wheel in the background and the lights of another amusement ride on the right. This was Marty's Bandstand. He set it up, the band played on . . . (Photograph courtesy of Mario Votolato.)

When times were very good, pre-World War II. The Spa at the intersection in Lower Simmons and Thornton was the mecca, part of a now primitive shopping "mall." Here proprietor Emil Fuoco, who was to go into the Army, stands proudly in his establishment. Notice the "seductive" girl hawking Camel cigarettes. (Photograph courtesy of Mary Fuoco.)

What a gang, and but for one, all alive and indeed kicking. Pictured are, from left to right, as follows: (front row) the late Mario Cardarelli, Billy Croce, and Carl Rainone; (second row) Joe Ricci and Raymond Iannuccilli; (third row) John ?, Frank Croce, and Mary Scungio; (back) Palma Scungio. This was a group that stuck together, all neighborhood "kids," virtually all from mill families. (Photograph courtesy of Palma De Blois.)

A John Street beauty standing against the cement block wall of a house in the mill village. Palma Scungio was raised in a row house, and was the daughter of Stacia, who worked in the mill. (Photograph courtesy of Palma De Blois.)

All assembled on a favorite rock. This family of three generations and a friend are at Goddard Park, the place to go for people of the villages. There were really only a couple of places that were frequented, this park and Oakland Beach, destroyed in the Hurricane of '38. Pictured here are Grandmother Menechelle Scungio, daughter-in-law Stacia Scungio (seated), who worked all her life in the Pocasset Mill, and Stacia's daughters Palma, Margaret, and behind her, Mary. The little girl with her arms about her knees was the next door neighbor, Nina Santurri. (Photograph courtesy of Palma De Blois.)

Another pre-Christmas party of women mill workers from the Priscilla Mills. Not the solitary man (on the left). This is the 1940s. (Photograph courtesy of Marian Crudale.)

Joe Croce himself, a strapping teenager, at his uncle Joe Barone's gas station in 1947. Behind him is the slope of Plainfield Pike, which led away from the town to a number of great farms and one of the most magnificent reservoirs in America. (Photograph courtesy of Joe Croce.)

A few nieces and an aunt at a mill house on John Street. Notice the row houses in the background. Here Annie Scungio proudly guards or shows off her nieces. (Photograph courtesy of Palma De Blois.)

An anticipated event in the streets of Olneyville. It was a visiting dignitary who created such a stir in the mill village. (Photograph courtesy of the Nickerson Community Center.)

Two Thornton-ites at the famous intersection of Atwood Avenue and Plainfield Street on a sunny, fall afternoon. They look like movie tough guys, but they aren't—it was a look cultivated in the 1940s. Actors like George Raft had something to do with it. (Photograph courtesy of Mario Votolato.)

The umpteenth birthday of a friend. How many of these women now called Senior Citizens worked in Olneyville Mills? Probably all of them. They certainly share many memories of those factory days. (Photograph courtesy of the Nickerson Community Center.)

Another outdoor gathering in Olneyville in the shadow of the Atlantic Mills. Gatherings like this became common, and outdoor flea markets are still very much in vogue. (Photograph courtesy of the Nickerson Community Center.)

Mary Fuoco in the family store at the intersection of Atwood and Plainfield. One would not call the war time a good time, but it certainly was a time of prosperity and for those left at home, the work was one of devotion. Here wife Mary makes a symbol of some kind, probably her own symbol of victory. She ran the store while her husband Emil was in the Army. Notice the prices of sundaes behind her. To go, you added 2¢! (Photograph courtesy of Mary Fuoco.)

Seven

Illustrious People

Hiram Kimball (right) and Hiram Jr., his son. Hiram ran the town, practically. He was, during the heyday of the mills, the dog catcher, chief of police, etc. for villages including Lower Simmonsville, Hughesdale, Thornton, Western Olneyville, Pocasset, etc. The town of Johnston was really his. He even ran for public office. Behind them is Dalton's, as it was called, and the sign behind the clerk says Crisco. Everybody cooked with Crisco in those days. (Photograph courtesy of Mario Votolato.)

The big band, and it played on and on. The town resident band, which played at marches in the mill villages, festivals, religious feasts, etc., was founded by Mr. Ferri, patriarch of the famous clan. In 1923, this was a musical group to be respected. (Photograph courtesy of Mary Fuoco.)

Hiram Kimball Jr., a chip off the old block to be sure. Like his illustrious dad, Hiram Jr. was a policeman and a member of one of the oldest English families in the area. The Kimballs "ran" the villages of Simmonsville, Thornton, Pocassett, etc. Hiram Jr. died at a very advanced age. (Photograph courtesy of Mario Votolato.)

Beautiful, patrician, and influential. Lyra Brown Nickerson, daughter of a very wealthy family, is shown here in a photograph from about 1853. Because of her efforts, the settlement house in Olneyville, in the true shadow of the great mills, became a reality. The building on the corner of Delaine and Appleton Streets became a great community center that remains vitally alive to this day. (Photograph courtesy of the Nickerson Community Center.)

The greatest house in four villages. This is the way the Simmons House looked on old Plainfield Street, lined with magnificent trees, in 1910. James Fowler Simmons was a senator, and he built this Greek Revival-style mansion about 1840. Simmons owned cotton mills in Simmonsville, Thornton, Hughesdale, Lower Simmons, etc., and these contributed to the growth of every one of the villages.

A most illustrious family of women (the sons are out of the picture for the moment). Mrs. Votolato and her daughters were tradition breakers, innovators, and progressive spirits. The Myrtle Theatre was theirs and in the early days of films Mrs. Votolato sold penny candy from a small booth at the rear of the theatre. One daughter was a nurse, and two were WACS. Mrs. Votolato lived into her nineties. (Photograph courtesy of Mario Votolato.)

The well-known Ferri house. Though perhaps not opulent by some standards, it must be remembered that decades ago, this was considered almost a mansion. The wealthiest and most influential family in the entire town lived here. Across the street was the magnificent Simmons House. The Ferri and Pezzulo families reigned long after the vanishing of that initial hardy breed, the English who built the mills and contributed to the wealth of later families. (Photograph courtesy of Mary Fuoco.)

Mary Ferri on her graduation from high school. Renowned for her beautiful skin, she was one of the first of the villages to go on to college and become a teacher. (Photograph courtesy of Mary Fuoco.)

The mighty Ferri clan. In the center is the matriarch, Nicolina Ferri, who established the family as one of the most prominent in the mill villages, from Simmonsville to Olneyville. They have assembled here on the stage of Ferri Hall, later to become a motion picture theatre. Included are sons, a daughter, in-laws, and grandchildren. (Photograph courtesy of Mary Fuoco.)

The great mansion, one hundred years ago. The Simmons mansion, bought by the prominent Pezzullo family, has been magnificently restored. Two of the Pezzullo children, Rita Saccoccio and Edmund Pezzullo, still reside in this historic mansion. (Photograph courtesy of Rita Saccoccio.)

The very beautiful Theresa De Sisto early in the 1900s. She married the prominent Joseph Pezzullo, state senator. (Photograph courtesy of Rita Saccoccio.)

A most illustrious and successful entrepreneur. Joseph Pezzullo was a contractor, businessman, state representative, and state senator from Johnston. He bought the great Simmons House and raised his large family there. (Photograph courtesy of Rita Saccoccio.)

The elegant wedding of Joseph Pezzullo and Theresa De Sisto. In 1921, the couple bought the great Simmons House and lived there all their lives. Behind the couple is Santo "Sally" De Sisto and Marie Pezzullo, who also married. Thus, the brother of the bride married the sister of the groom. (Photograph courtesy of Rita Saccoccio.)

Eight
Yesterday and Today

The great Atlantic Mills of Olneyville today. The domes are intact, but broken. The mill is now home to flea markets, private small businesses, etc. (Photograph by Albert J. Lothrop.)

The last intact remaining mill house in Simmonsville-Hughesdale. Privately owned, it retains much of its two-hundred-year-old character. (Photograph by Albert J. Lothrop.)

The Victoria Mill of today, its windows largely sealed, its industry vanished. (Photograph by Albert J. Lothrop.)

The interior of the Priscilla Mill. This is the way it was—and will likely never be again. Now empty, try to picture it in the days when it teemed with men and women working ten to twelve hours a day, sometimes longer. They have left their marks in such rooms. (Photograph courtesy of Joe Fuoco.)

Two buddies, two avenues in life. George Del Santo (left) became one of the village's very few early insurance brokers. The man to the right, Joe Fuoco Sr., was a mill worker most of his life. They are both gone—yesterday they were a part of the mill town, today a part of the legend. (Photograph courtesy of Joe Fuoco.)

Workers in one of the small mills of Simmons Lower/Thornton village. Here the cloth was cut by hand, and suits carefully assembled. From the very old to the very young, all worked in this room. (Photograph courtesy of Viola La Chapelle.)

A fitting end, perhaps, to a way of work and a way of life. This photograph is of a nearly completely obscured stone mill in Simmonsville. Destroyed by the Great Flood of April 13, 1840, it stands a ruin today, a memory, a relic. (Photograph by Albert J. Lothrop.)